First, We Sing!
Digital Resource Supplements
For Planning & Assessment

By Susan Brumfield

DIGITAL DOWNLOAD CODE
To access DIGITAL CONTENT, go to:
www.halleonard.com/mylibrary

Enter Code
2355-2207-9887-8084

This publication is intended for use by one school or organization only. All data files are for teacher planning and assessment use only. No other part of this publication may be reproduced or distributed in any form or by any means without the prior written permission of the Publisher.

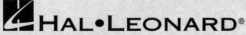

7777 W. BLUEMOUND RD. P.O. BOX 13819 MILWAUKEE, WI 53213

In Australia Contact:
Hal Leonard Australia Pty. Ltd.
4 Lentara Court
Cheltenham, Victoria, 3192 Australia
Email: ausadmin@halleonard.com.au

Copyright © 2017 by HAL LEONARD LLC
International Copyright Secured   All Rights Reserved

Visit Hal Leonard Online at
www.halleonard.com

Table of Contents

Introduction 3
Digital Download Content 4

Digital Tools for Planning

Templates for Song Analysis & Lesson Planning . . . 6
Activity Cards 9
Digital Supplements for Teaching Strategies 10

Digital Tools for Assessment

Assessment in the Kodály-Inspired Classroom . . . 12
Checklist for Concept Readiness & Mastery 14
Activity Card Assessment Rubrics 15
Skill Development Assessment Rubrics 16
Additional Resources and References 18
Digital Library of Rhythmic Element Images . . . 19

About the Writer 20

Acknowledgments

Special thanks to Beth Berridge, for providing both administrative and pedagogical insights in developing the format and content of the assessment documents, and to Jim Gent, for lending creative vision, technical expertise and practical teaching experience in creating the digital assets and their "how-to" instructions for *First, We Sing!* Thanks also to the many music teachers and Kodály summer course students who have offered ideas and suggested content for the digital supplement.

As always, I am grateful to the creative design team at Hal Leonard, and to Emily Crocker for her ongoing encouragement and support. Most especially, I would like to thank Myra Murray, Senior Editor for Classroom Publications, for her wisdom, experience, patience and humor throughout the process of bringing our vision for *First, We Sing!* to reality.

Introduction

Welcome! If you've been using the *First, We Sing!* Kodály-inspired curriculum in your classroom, you're already familiar with its components:

- Teacher Guide (Hal Leonard #00118549)
- Teaching Strategies for Rhythmic and Melodic Elements: Primary Grades (Hal Leonard #00127715)
- Teaching Strategies for Rhythmic and Melodic Elements: Intermediate Grades (Hal Leonard #00140886)
- Practice Activity Cards (Hal Leonard #00127714)
- *First, We Sing!* Songbooks (Hal Leonard #09971663, #00145629, #00234061)

The *First, We Sing!* materials were created for novice and experienced teachers alike, to offer guidance and direction for teachers who are new to the Kodály approach, as well as to provide useful ideas and tools to help streamline planning and delivery of instruction. If you're new to the *First, We Sing!* series, you'll want to start by purchasing the print materials listed above.

We're dedicated to the development of helpful, practical supplemental and ancillary materials that support this inspiring and creative way of teaching. The *FWS Digital Resource Supplements* is an exciting resource, filled with a variety of terrific teacher planning and assessment tools for implementing the *First, We Sing!* curriculum in your K-5 classes. You'll find everything you need to create electronic versions of the tools you use every day.

Digital Tools for Assessment

Designed to complement curriculum materials from the *FWS Teaching Guide, Teaching Strategies* and *Activity Cards*, these digital templates are easy to use for practical and efficient assessment of both group and individual progress. Using rubrics and checklists, you can:

- modify the *sequence* to include rhythmic and melodic elements that *you* choose to teach at each grade level.
- keep track of your students' progression through the "three-step process" (*preparation, presentation* and *practice*) of each element.
- track your students' growth and development of musical skills through assessment of selected *preparation* and *practice activities*.
- record individual and class progress toward achieving yearly goals from the *scope and sequence* for each grade.

How to Get Started

These tools are flexible; if you're tech-savvy, feel free to jump in with both feet. If not, don't worry! This supplement comes with teacher-tested, easy-to-follow instructions that will walk you through the set-up process, step by step. Take your time and start with the pieces you find most immediately useful. There are so many great features from which to choose! You'll quickly find what you're looking for, because there are handy references to the print materials throughout.

What is available with the Digital Download?

Digital Tools For Planning

- **Planning Templates**
  - Song Analysis Template
  - 6 Sample Yearly Plans (one for each grade level K-5)
  - Daily Lesson Plan
- **130 Activity Cards**
- **Digital Supplements for Teaching Strategies**
  - Step-by-Step Instructions to build 36 presentation slides for all rhythmic and melodic elements presented in primary and intermediate grades.
  - Over 150 images of music notation "snips" and graphics

Digital Tools For Assessment

- 36 Checklists for Concept Readiness and Mastery
- Activity Card Assessment Rubrics
- 47 Skill Development Assessment Rubrics
- Image Library of 19 rhythm notation symbols

How to Access the Digital Content

1. To access content in Hal Leonard's MY LIBRARY, go to www.halleonard.com/mylibrary.

2. Follow the instructions to set up your own My Library account (if you haven't already done so). This way, codes are saved for future access, and you don't have to re-enter them each time.

3. Once you have created your own library account, then enter the 16-digit product code listed on page 1 of the book. The digital content will then be added to your My Library account.

4. Locate the product cover image and click to open. You will see 2 main content folders:
   - Digital Tools for Planning
   - Digital Tools for Assessment

Inside these folders, you will find are a variety of PDF and image files. The PDF files may be viewed in My Library and/or downloaded to your computer. The image files are in zipped folders and must be downloaded. See page 5 for instructions.

> **Important:** Follow these instructions to **properly** download, unzip and open these zipped files. We suggest using one of the following browsers: **Chrome** or **Firefox**.

Windows Users: Download Content from Zip Folders

When you are ready to download content from **Hal Leonard MY LIBRARY**, please note that every file called a **"regular zipfile"** is in a "zip folder" format. Downloading and using the content in a zip folder requires a few additional steps.

1. In your Hal Leonard MY LIBRARY account, click on "download" next to the zip file you'd like to access.

2. Wait while your computer downloads a zip folder. This should only take a few minutes.

3. Once the zip folder is done downloading, access your downloads folder. To access this folder, click on the "Windows" icon on the bottom left corner of your screen, then select "computer" from that menu, then select "downloads."

4. Find the zip folder you just downloaded. The folder name should correspond to what it is called in "My Library."

5. Select and RIGHT CLICK on the zip file. Select "extract" or "extract all."

6. Click on "browse," select "desktop" for your destination, then click "OK" and "extract." Your computer will take a few minutes to extract the bigger files from this smaller, condensed zip folder.

7. Once it is finished extracting the files, locate this folder on your desktop. Remember, the folder name should correspond to what it is called in "My Library."

8. Double click on this folder to open it.

Mac Users: Download Content from Zip Folders

When you are ready to download content from **Hal Leonard MY LIBRARY**, please note that every file called a **"regular zipfile"** is in a "zip folder" format. Downloading and using the content in a zip folder requires a few additional steps.

1. In your Hal Leonard MY LIBRARY account, click on "download" next to the zip file you'd like to access.

2. Wait while your computer downloads a zip folder. This should only take a few minutes.

3. Once the zip folder is done downloading, access your downloads folder. To access your downloads folder, go to the bottom left corner of your screen, into the dock. Your downloads folder should be located here. Find the zip folder you just downloaded. The folder name should correspond to what it is called in MY LIBRARY.

4. Click on and drag the zip folder to your desktop. Double click on this zip folder. By doing this, your computer is extracting the bigger files from this smaller, condensed zip folder.

5. Double click on the new folder to open it.

Digital Tools for Planning

Planning Templates

For grade level objectives, song analysis, yearly plans and daily lesson plans – use "as is" or customize to fit your own sequence. Add links to recordings, videos and other digital materials, and keep your lesson files at your fingertips.

- ***Song Analysis Template***

    (Interactive PDF that correlates to *FWS Teacher Guide* pp. 81-82)

- ## K-5 Sample Yearly Plans
  (PDFs by grade level that correlate to *FWS Teacher Guide* pp. 75-77)

FIRST GRADE YEARLY PLAN

Grade 1	September	October	November	December	January	February	March	April	May
Review K concepts	•••••	•••••	•••••	•••••	•••••	•••••	•••••	•••••	•••••
Beat / Rhythms	>>>>>*•••	•••••	•••••	•••••	•••••	•••••	•••••	•••••	•••••
♩ ♫		>>>>>>>>	>>>*•••	•••••	•••••	•••••	•••••	•••••	•••••
𝄽 (rest)		>>>>>>>>	>>>>>*••	>>>*•••	•••••	•••••	•••••	•••••	•••••

so & mi
  solfa notation
  handsigns
	>>>>>>>>	>>>>>>>>	>>>>>>>>	>>>>>>>>	>>>>*•••	•••••	•••••	•••••	•••••

Staff
  lines and spaces
  one-line
  three-line
  five-line
						*••••	•••••	•••••	•••••

2 meter
  barlines
  measures
  conducting in 2
	>>>>>>>>	>>>>>>>>	>>>>>>>>	>>>>>>>>	>>>>>>>>	>>>*•••	•••••	•••••	•••••

la *so-la* (M2)	>>>>>>>>	>>>>>>>>	>>>>>>>>	>>>>>>>>	>>>>>>>>	>>>>>>>>	>>>*•••	•••••	•••••
Repeat sign	>>>>>>>>	>>>>>>>>	>>>>>>>>	>>>>>>>>	>>>>>>>>	>>>>>>>>	>>>>>>>>	>>>*•••	•••••

SECOND GRADE YEARLY PLAN

Grade 2	September	October	November	December	January	February	March	April	May
Review Grade 1*	•••••	•••••	•••••	•••••	•••••	•••••	•••••	•••••	•••••
Known notes in new motives: (*la* in *mi –la* turn)	>>>>*•••	•••••	•••••	•••••	•••••	•••••	•••••	•••••	•••••

do
  so mi do
  so - do
  do - clef
  (F, C, and C - *do*)
  ledger line
	>>>>>>>>	>>>*•••	•••••	•••••	•••••	•••••	•••••	•••••	•••••

♫♫	>>>>>>>>	>>>>>>>>	>>>*•••	•••••	•••••	•••••	•••••	•••••	•••••

re
  mi re do
  (F, C and C - *do*)
	>>>>>>>>	>>>>>>>>	>>>>>>>>	>>>>>>>>	>>>>*•••	•••••	•••••	•••••	•••••

Staff hand staff						>>>>>*••	•••••	•••••	•••••

4 meter
  barlines
  measures
  conducting in 4
				>>>>>>>>	>>>>>>>>	>>>>*•••	•••••	•••••	•••••

♩♩ = 𝅗𝅥					>>>>>>>>	>>>>>>>>	>>>*•••	•••••	•••••
First and second endings								>>>*•••	•••••

Digital Tools for Planning

- *Daily Lesson Plan*

    (Interactive PDF that correlates to *FWS Teacher Guide* p. 78)

Digital Activity Cards

Practice activities provide fast, fun and creative ways to give students a workout in each of the six skill areas: reading, writing, part-work, memory, listening and creating. Now in digital form, individual activity cards can be sorted, selected and saved for easy access. Copy, drag and drop the .png images into folders for specific lessons, or just browse the digital "card file" for ideas.

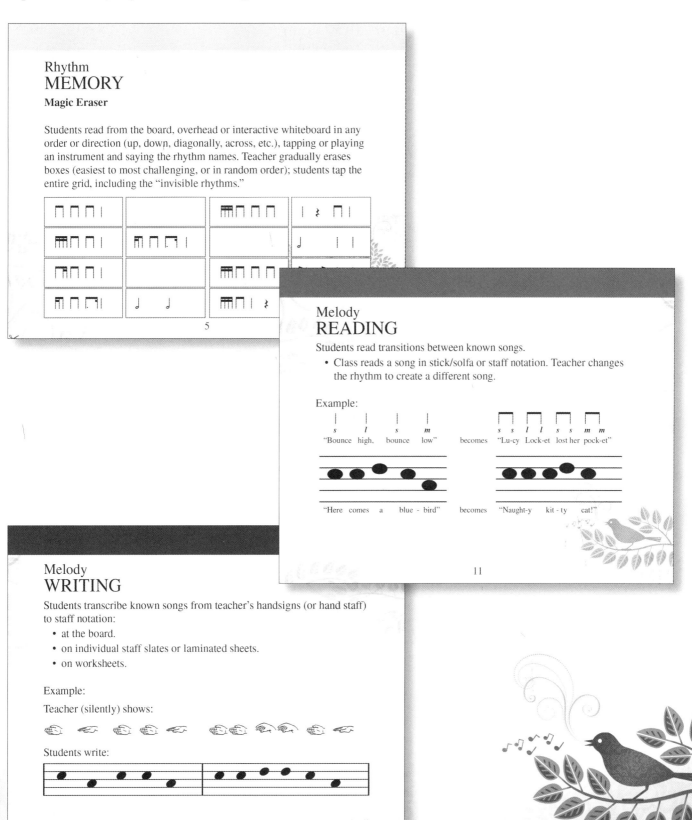

Digital Tools for Planning

Digital Supplements for Teaching Strategies

- *Lesson Slide Contents*

    What should be included on each slide? The manipulatives provided directly correspond to each of the steps in an element's presentation lesson. **Create a slide that works for *your* classroom.** Realistically, if you don't create a slide that is easy for *you* to use, you won't use it. Work within your knowledge base and explore ways that these items can be used to aid *your* teaching. The slide setups describe the purpose for the creation of each manipulative.

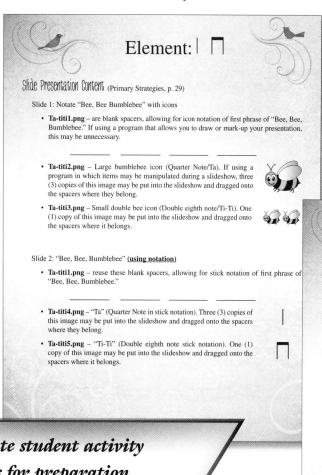

Teacher-friendly, step-by-step instructions make it easy to customize the content for use with your preferred presentation platform.

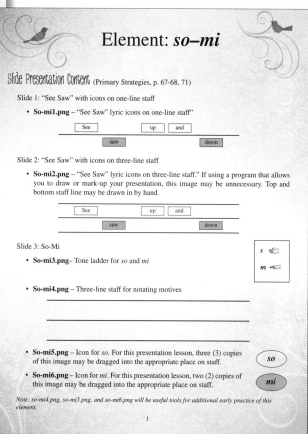

Create student activity slides for preparation, presentation and practice lessons in the primary and intermediate grades.

- **Choose a Presentation Medium**

The most beneficial use of these materials for the purposes of presenting the curriculum will come from a format in which the items may be moved and manipulated during a presentation. Below is a list of mediums that have proven effective and ways to use them, based on the availability of technology in your classroom:

SMART Boards, Promethean Boards, other Interactive Whiteboards or Tablet-based presentation apps: Explain Everything™, Doceri®, Educreations, (etc)

- These tend to be the most effective methods, if you have access to the technology. Slides can be actively displayed and manipulated and/or marked up easily using the touchscreen.

PowerPoint™ and Keynote®

- These methods are less effective, but they can still be used with the files. While objects like noteheads and icons cannot be manipulated during an active presentation, these methods provide a base for the presentation. Projection onto a whiteboard or chalkboard instead of a screen allows for a combination of virtual and physical manipulatives. Alternatively, these programs have 'mark-up' options during a live presentation. A similar effect can be achieved using a drawing tablet or mouse.

Printed Versions/Transparencies

- If projection through computer-based programs is not an option, consider formatting these images in a word processor and printing them in large, laminated copies or transparency format that can then be manipulated or projected on an overhead projector.

How to Store Images

- If using a computer to create your presentation lesson, store the images in an easy-to-access location.
- If using a portable device, these files will need to be transferred to the device directly (refer to your devices instructions for transferring photos to your device) or stored remotely (Google Drive™, Dropbox™ iCloud®, Amazon® Cloud Drive, etc.).

Includes a full image library of over 150 music notation "snips" and graphics designed for use with your tablet, computer or interactive whiteboard.

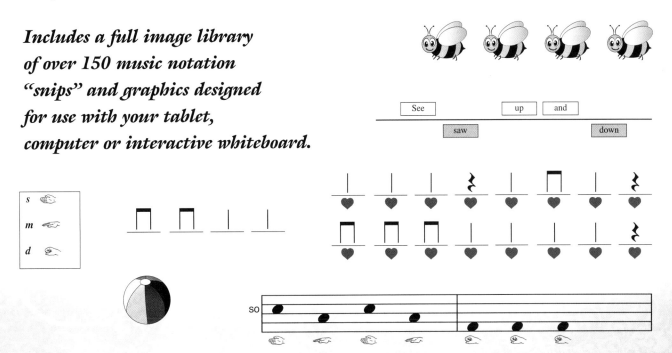

Digital Tools for Assessment

Assessment in the Kodály-Inspired Classroom

"A child should not collect concepts and definitions, but the treasures of music. There will be plenty of time to evaluate, arrange and review them later." [1]

Zoltan Kodály

What's the purpose of assessment in the music class?

Good teachers know that assessment is an essential part of effective teaching and successful learning. Teachers plan and deliver instruction based on their curricular choices, and rely on informal procedural activities and formal assessment of their students' skills to evaluate the degree of its success. They use the information they collect to analyze, reflect and, when necessary, revise the instruction in an on-going cycle of teaching and learning.

This process is inherent in much of the music-making that occurs in classrooms and rehearsals every day. But in an educational climate which often values testing and measuring data for its own sake, music teachers are frustrated by what seems to be an extra layer of seemingly pointless paperwork. Unfortunately, assessment in music is often limited to quizzes on historical facts and theoretical information ("lines and spaces of the treble clef," etc.), and other easy-to-measure aspects. Emerging musical skills and aesthetic factors like satisfaction and enjoyment are less quantifiable and can be more difficult to evaluate. Constantly evolving local, state and national standards make it difficult to know what to assess, and with large classes and limited time, even the most committed professionals struggle to balance planning and teaching with testing and reporting. Despite these challenges, today's teachers are moving beyond traditional "pencil and paper" tests and seeking creative ways to assess the multiple "ways of knowing" their students are experiencing through music.

Making Assessment Count

Dr. Scott C. Schuler, a former president of NAfME and expert on assessment in music education, suggests that assessment should (a) enhance learning, (b) improve teaching, (c) improve the instructional program and (d) inform "stake-holders" (students, parents and policy-makers).[2] In addition to helping students grow and succeed, effective assessment can play an important role in advocacy for music education in schools.

There are several types of assessment, all of which inform teachers, students and parents in different ways.

- *Diagnostic, or baseline assessment* helps teachers determine the starting point for instruction. This type of activity is necessary to determine student *readiness* for new learning.
- *Formative assessment* is designed to provide feedback to both teacher and students during the course of instruction. It may be as informal as observing the students in action during class, or it can be more structured. Generally geared toward the assessment of *progress* toward instructional goals, this type of assessment often includes specific guidance and steps toward improvement.

---

1 Ildikó Herboly Kocsár, ed., *Music Should Belong to Everyone: 120 Quotations from His Writings and Speeches* (Budapest, International Kodály Society, 2002), 53.
2 S.C. Schuler, "Music Assessment, Part 1: What and Why," *Music Educators Journal* 98 (2) (2011):10-13.

- *Summative assessment* occurs near the end of the learning process and allows teachers to observe the level of mastery of a skill, or understanding of a concept at a given time.

Ultimately, assessments provide the information needed to *evaluate* the students' achievement in relation to an age or grade-level expectation. *Grading* is another complex issue, which may or may not be linked to actual proficiency, along with effort, participation and conduct in the music class.[3]

Assessment and the Kodály Approach

Some teachers view assessment as a "fourth" step in the "three-step process" of *preparation, presentation* and *practice,* as many formal assessment activities do occur during the late practice stage. In reality, the teacher observes the students' skills as they work sequentially through each of the preparation and practice activities. Often underestimated or overlooked entirely, these tiny "steps within the steps" are crucial to the students' success. In a Kodály-inspired *spiral* curriculum, the successful mastery of one concept or skill can indicate readiness for the next step. In this way, it is possible for an assessment activity to serve multiple purposes.[4]

Assessment Tools

Assessment tools should be efficient and easy to use so that they can be implemented frequently and consistently. *Checklists, rating scales* and *rubrics* can help teachers keep their instructional goals in mind, and can provide information about the "next step" in student learning. They may also be used as "artifacts," along with recordings, videos and self-reflections, to comprise individual yearly *portfolios* for each student.

---

[3] Patricia Shehan Campbell, *Musician and Teacher: An Orientation to Music Education* (New York, NY 2008), 253-259.
[4] For an overview of the Kodály-inspired "three-step process, see pages 12-16 in *"First, We Sing! Teacher Guide.*

Digital Tools for Assessment

- ### *Checklist for Concept Readiness and Mastery*

  This *interactive checklist* format is designed to help you implement the "three-step process" *(preparation, presentation, practice)* into your teaching of rhythmic and melodic elements. With one element per page, each checklist correlates to the *FWS Teaching Strategies* and includes a handy page reference for the corresponding *presentation* procedure, along with a summary of preparation and practice activities. Keep these "to-do" lists with your planning materials to ensure that your students are ready to move from one step in the process to the next.

- ## *Activity Card Assessment Rubrics*

The biggest obstacle most teachers face in collecting and reporting assessment data is that the procedures cut into already-limited teaching time. That's why it's important that assessment takes place within the activities already happening in your lessons. The good news: *First, We Sing!* preparation and practice cards are easy to use as assessment activities!

By including these quick, fun activities in each lesson, you can assess group readiness to move on with concepts and skills. Use the *interactive activity card assessment rubrics* to collect and document information on both group or individual work. The level of mastery can be noted using a number scale (*0 – 3+ errors*), or you can customize the rubric parameters to fit your preferred indicators. You can modify the activities (and the rubrics) for students who need more time, extra help or even extra challenge. And because the practice activities are grouped (and color coded) by skill, it's possible to get a sense of your students' strengths and challenges over time.

STUDENT: Jarrett Smith		GRADE: 4th		CLASS: Anderson			
ACTIVITY CARD	**SKILL AREA**	**RHYTHM or MELODY**	**ELEMENT**	0 errors	1 error	2 errors	3+ errors
Rhythm Det.	Reading	Rhythm	♩ ♪ ♪				

STUDENT:		GRADE:		CLASS:			
ACTIVITY CARD	**SKILL AREA**	**RHYTHM or MELODY**	**ELEMENT**	0 errors	1 error	2 errors	3+ errors

Digital Tools for Assessment

- **Skill Development Assessment Rubrics**

While some music teachers are expected to adhere to national, state or district standards, others are completely on their own when it comes to curricular decision-making. One thing most teachers agree on: there is never enough time when it comes to active music-making in the classroom. We want students to have opportunities to sing, play, move, explore, listen, compose and improvise, and we also want them to learn to read and notate music. We want them to experience folk music, art music and music of many world cultures. And we often have less than thirty minutes a week to make sure we fit it all in. Let's face it: it's just not possible to do everything in every lesson, every day, with every grade level.

That's where the expertise of the teacher comes in: YOU decide what experiences are most meaningful for the students in YOUR particular setting, at any particular time. Hopefully, you're able to lead your students through a world of diverse musical opportunities, encompassing all skill areas from performing to literacy. But you may choose to prioritize when it comes to assessing and reporting those skills, depending on how often you see your students. That's why each page of the *skill development assessment rubric* includes descriptors of the musical task. Use these forms to assess and record progress in all skill areas, or choose one or two as your focus for the year. You can document the growth of individual students, or the class as a whole (making note of students whose skills are above or below the average of the group).

Record students' progress in each area of musical skill.

Here's a sample rubric key:

○   Needs remediation of requisite readiness skills for this task.

⊟   Did not successfully complete the musical task at this time.

◪   Shows improvement and/or progress toward mastery of the musical task.

√   Demonstrates proficient performance of the musical task in various contexts of complexity or difficulty; ready for the next step.

\#   Demonstrates an exceptionally high level of mastery in this skill area (beyond grade level expectation), ready for a new challenge.

☐   (N/A) Did not assess

Remember, musical skills are developmental, and they don't necessarily unfold at the same rate for every student. There are also other factors to consider, such as ESL students, students with exceptionalities, and lack of experience or inconsistency in instruction on previous grade levels. Taking "snapshots" of your students' growth at the beginning, in the middle and at the end of the year is a great way to document their progress over time. The suggested skill level for students in each grade aligns with the grade level objectives in the Teaching Guide of the *First, We Sing!* Curriculum (pp.52-70). These curricular guidelines offer a platform for communication with your administrators, colleagues, and parents about the possibilities for musical achievement, given adequate time and resources.

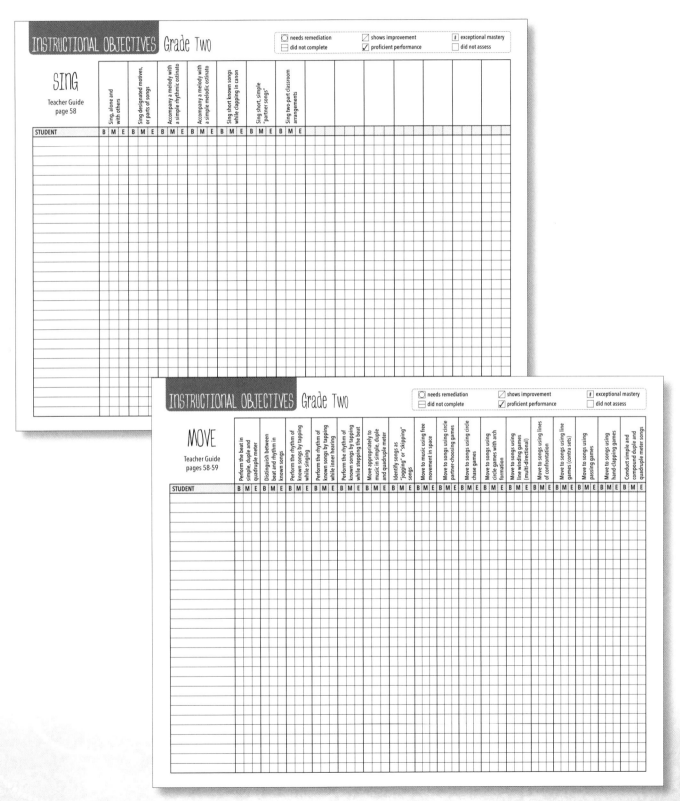

Additional Resources and References

Brophy, Timothy S. *Assessing the Developing Child Musician*. Chicago, IL: GIA Publications, Inc., 2010.

Brophy, Timothy S. (ed.) *Assessment in Music Education: Framework, Models and Designs*. Chicago, IL: GIA Publications, Inc., 2010.

Campbell, Patricia Shehan. *Musician and Teacher: An Orientation to Music Education*. New York, NY: W.W. Norton & Co., 2008.

Conway, Colleen (ed.) *Musicianship-Focused Curriculum and Assessment*. Chicago, IL: GIA Publications, Inc., 2015.

Durairaj, Manju. *Interact with Music Assessment (Levels 1 & 2)*. Milwaukee, WI: Hal Leonard Music, 2014.

Fautley, Martin. *Assessment in Music Education*. New York, NY: Oxford University Press, 2010.

Kocsár, Ildikó Herboly (ed.). *Music Should Be for Everyone: 120 Quotations from Kodaly's Speeches*, trans. Lilli Vandulek. Budapest: International Kodály Society, 2002.

Schuler, Scott C. "Music Assessment, Part 1: What and Why." *Music Educators Journal* 98 (2), 2011.

Wilkins, Bryan M. "Assessment & the National Standards in the Kodály Context." Presentation at the OAKE Western Division Conference, Portland, OR, October 12, 2013.

Digital Library of Rhythmic Element Images

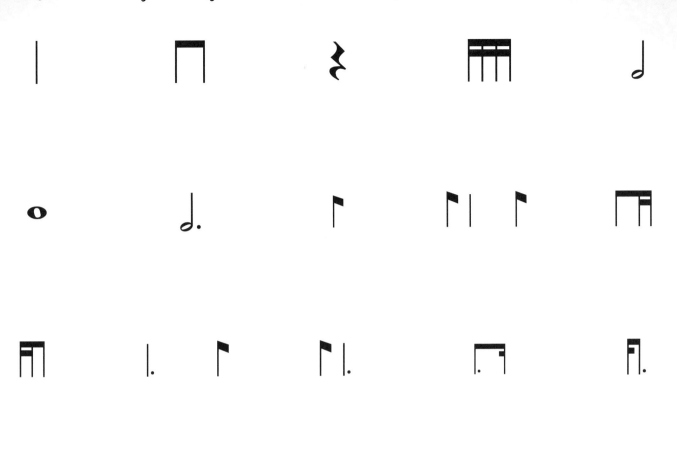

First, We Sing! Digital Resource Supplements

About the Writer

Dr. Susan Brumfield is Professor of Music Education at Texas Tech University, and holds a Ph.D. in Music Education from the University of Oklahoma. She is known throughout the United States and Europe as a clinician, consultant, author, composer, arranger and conductor of children's choirs, and is an internationally recognized Kodály educator. Dr. Brumfield is the author of *First, We Sing! Kodály-Inspired Teaching in the Music Classroom* (Hal Leonard), a set of Kodály-based curriculum and resource materials for K-5 music.

Dr. Brumfield's other publications include *Hot Peas and Barley-O: Children's Songs and Games from Scotland* and *Over the Garden Wall: Children's Songs and Games from England*. She recently completed *Kentucky Mother Goose*, with American folk legend Jean Ritchie, and is currently working on *Giro Giro Tondo: Children's Songs and Games from Italy*. Dr. Brumfield is a contributing author for *Music Express Magazine* and McGraw Hill's *Music Studio*.

Founder and Artistic Director of The West Texas Children's Chorus, Dr. Brumfield is also in frequent demand as a commissioned composer. Dr. Brumfield's choral music is published with Hal Leonard Music, Colla Voce Music and BriLee/Carl Fischer. Dr. Brumfield was honored in both 2012 and 2014 with the Texas Tech University College of Visual and Performing Arts Award for Outstanding Research, and as a two-time finalist for the President's Book Award.